W9-ARW-803

Hoppin' Magic

My First
String & Knot
MAGIC
TRICKS

Written by Stephanie Johnson

Illustrated by Kerry Manwaring

SMITHMARK

Mend the Rope

How does a cut rope mend itself? It's magic!

What You'll Need:

♦ A 2-foot piece of rope and a 1-foot piece of rope
◊ Sharp scissors ♦ Glue

Getting Ready:

1. Glue the ends of the long rope together to create a loop. Do this neatly so that it is hard to tell where the rope was glued together. Let the glue dry overnight.

2. Put the short rope through the long rope and glue the two ends of the short rope together.

3. With your left hand, hold the long rope near the spot where it was glued together. Then, bunch up the short rope so it's hidden in your left hand.

NOTE TO PARENTS

Although every magic trick in this book has been kid-tested, and can, with practice, be easily performed by most children, some tricks are more difficult than others and may require your supervision. Please read every trick before allowing your child to do it. The RGA Publishing Group and SMITHMARK Publishers will not be held responsible for any injury that occurs during the practice or performance of a trick.

An RGA Book

Copyright © 1992 by RGA Publishing Group, Inc.
This edition published in 1992 by SMITHMARK Publishers, Inc.,
112 Madison Avenue, New York, NY 10016.
Manufactured in the United States of America.
SMITHMARK Books are available for bulk purchase for sales promotion and premium use. For details write or telephone the Manager of Special Sales, SMITHMARK Publishers, Inc., 112 Madison Avenue, New York, NY 10016; (212) 532-6600.

ISBN 0-8317-6241-1

Doing the Trick:

1. Show the loop to your audience and say, "I have here an ordinary loop of rope."

2. Then pick up the scissors and say, "I will now cut the rope." Cut the rope exactly in the place where it was glued together.

3. With your right hand, hold up one of the cut ends, and bring your hands together in front of you and pause. *The short rope should still be hidden in your left hand.*

4. Then say, "I will now magically mend the rope!" Pull your hands apart suddenly, sliding the short rope off the long rope with a quick tug. In the same motion, drop the long rope to the floor. *Do not let your audience see you drop the long rope.*

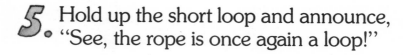

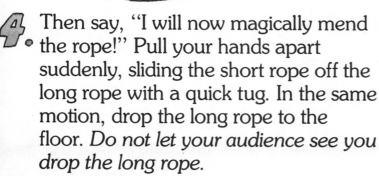

5. Hold up the short loop and announce, "See, the rope is once again a loop!"

Where's the Middle?

Here's a tricky stunt that will fool your friends and family!

What You'll Need:

- A 6-foot length of rope
- A pencil (or your magic wand)

Getting Ready:

1. Fold the rope in half. Then roll it up into a coil and lay it on the floor. You will see two tear-shaped spaces, one is actually the middle of the rope, the other is not.

2. The object of this trick is to fool your audience into believing that you know which is really the middle of the rope. Study the tear-shaped spaces well, and practice this trick several times.

Doing the Trick:

1. Ask a volunteer from the audience to come onstage. Use the pencil or magic wand to point out the two tear shapes. Say, "One of these spaces is the middle of the rope."

2. Have the volunteer point to the space that he or she thinks is the middle. If your volunteer points to the *wrong* space, pull the two ends of the rope together to uncoil the rope and show the volunteer that he or she is wrong.

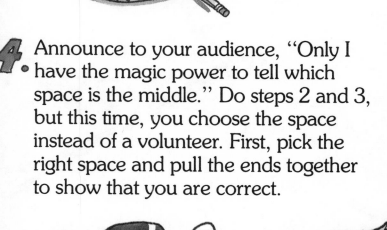

3. If the volunteer points to the *right* space, fool him or her by pulling the ends of the rope away from each other. Either way, the volunteer loses!

4. Announce to your audience, "Only I have the magic power to tell which space is the middle." Do steps 2 and 3, but this time, you choose the space instead of a volunteer. First, pick the right space and pull the ends together to show that you are correct.

5. Next choose the wrong space, but fool your audience by pulling the two ends away from each other. Either way you choose, you're right.

The Amazing Rope Escape

You'll make the impossible possible with this baffling escape stunt!

What You'll Need:

- ▲ Two 5-foot pieces of rope or cord
- ▲ A 6-inch piece of thread

Getting Ready:

1. Lay the ropes on the floor side to side. Use the thread to tie the two middles together as shown.

2. Bend the ends of one rope to the right, and the ends of the other rope to the left.

Doing the Trick:

1. Before showing the ropes to your audience, hold them in the middle so that your hand covers both the thread and the bends in the ropes.

2. Hold up the ropes and say, "I have in my hand two ropes." Ask for two volunteers to come onstage. Have one volunteer stand on your left and one stand on your right. Announce, "These two assistants will tie me up and I will escape."

3. Holding the folded ropes tightly, put them behind your back.

4. Tell the volunteers to grab the ropes closest to them. Have them bring the ropes around to the front and tie a single knot around your waist. Say, "I will hold the ropes up while you do this."

5. When the knot has been tied, ask each of the volunteers to pull on either side of the rope as shown. Say, "When I count to three, pull on the rope so the knot will get tighter."

6. Then count, "One, two, three!" When the volunteers pull, the thread will break and fall to the floor, unseen by the audience. You will be free!

Tricky Tailor

Here's a trick that will show your speed and skill!

What You'll Need:

- 2 buttons identical to the ones on the shirt you will wear during the trick
- Thread that matches the thread used to sew those buttons on your shirt
- A needle • Scissors

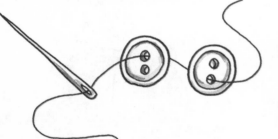

Getting Ready:

1. Thread the needle, then string the buttons onto the thread.

2. Tie the buttons back to back and cut the thread. When you have finished, keep the extra thread in the needle.

3. Unbutton one button on your shirt. Put one of the doubled buttons through the buttonhole. Smooth out the front of your shirt to make it look as though all the buttons were buttoned.

Doing the Trick:

1. Put the scissors, needle, and thread on your show table. Tell your audience that you have just taken a sewing class and you are now the fastest tailor in the world. Say, "I will now demonstrate my expert sewing skills."

2. Take the scissors and cut the doubled button off your shirt. Catch the button on the outside with your hand. The button on the inside will fall down into your shirt without being seen.

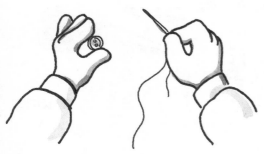

3. Show the button you cut off to your audience. Pick up the needle and thread in your free hand and say, "I will now instantly sew the button back on."

4. Turn around and say, "Abracadabra, alakazam!" While you are saying these words, quickly button your shirt with the real button that is already on your shirt. Drop the button in your hand onto the floor or put it in your pocket or into your shirt.

5. Then turn around and face your audience. Say, "Voilà! The fastest sewer in the world."

Two into One

ALAKAZAM, ALAKAZUM! I'LL MAKE THESE ROPES TURN INTO ONE!

Fascinate your friends and family by turning two ropes into one!

What You'll Need:

- A 24-inch piece of rope or cord
- Scissors

Getting Ready:

1. Cut the rope into one 8-inch-long piece and one 16-inch-long piece.

2. Wear a jacket or loose fitting pants with large pockets when performing this trick.

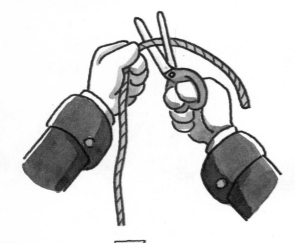

Doing the Trick:

1. Before you do the trick, bend each rope in half. Then, hold the ropes so that your hand covers the bends.

2. Show the ropes to your audience and say, "Here are two magic ropes." The ropes will look as if they were the same length.

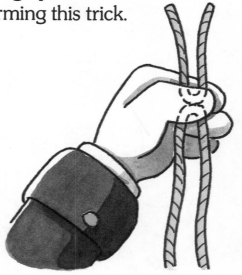

3. Announce, "I will now put the magic ropes into my pocket." Stuff the short rope into your jacket or pants pocket and let the two ends of the long rope hang over the edge of the pocket.

4. Wave your wand in the air and say, "Alakazam, alakazum! Make these ropes turn into one!"

5. Carefully pull on one of the long ends. Keep pulling until you have pulled the long rope completely out of your pocket. *Be careful not to pull out the short rope.*

6. Proudly tell your audience, "The two ropes have now become one!"

Swinging Bottle

MAGIC WAND, DO YOUR THING! MAKE THIS BOTTLE SWING AND SWING!

No one but you, the magician, can magically lift and swing a bottle using only a rope!

What You'll Need:

- ★ A plastic soda bottle
- ★ Black poster paint   ★ A paintbrush
- ★ A small rubber ball (the ball must be small enough to fit through the bottleneck opening, but no less than half the width of the bottleneck)
- ★ A 2-foot rope about ½-inch wide in diameter

Getting Ready:

1. Paint the soda bottle black.

2. Practice this trick enough to make sure the bottle and rope are the right size and length.

Doing the Trick:

1. Hide the ball in your pocket, up your sleeve, or in your hand. *Don't let your audience see it.*

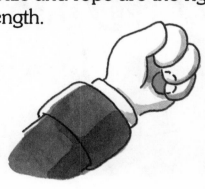

2. Put the bottle and rope on the show table. Ask for a volunteer from the audience. Tell the volunteer to stuff the rope into the bottle and then hold the bottle up by the rope. The volunteer won't be able to do it because the rope will keep coming out of the bottle.

3. When he or she has given up, take the bottle and rope and say, "I will now swing this empty bottle from this same piece of rope."

4. Stuff the rope into the bottle, then slip the ball in *without letting the audience see you do it.*

5. Now say, "Magic wand, do your thing. Make this bottle swing and swing!"

6. Turn the bottle upside down. Slowly pull on the rope until it catches on the ball inside. The ball, unseen by the audience, will hold the rope in the bottleneck.

7. Holding the rope tightly, turn the bottle upright. Be careful not to let the ball slip back down into the bottle. Then swing the bottle from the rope. Everyone will be surprised to see the bottle stay on the end of the rope!

Magic Spool

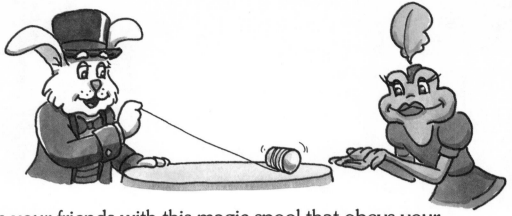

Amaze your friends with this magic spool that obeys your every wish!

What You'll Need:

- An unopened can of soup
- Masking tape
- A ball of string

Getting Ready:

1. Remove the label from the can, but do not open the can.

2. Tape the end of the string to the side of the can about one-quarter of an inch from the top edge. Wind the string around the can evenly from top to bottom to create a "spool."

Doing the Trick:

1. Lay the "spool" on its side. Tell your audience, "This is a magic spool of string that obeys my every command."

2. Hold the loose end of the string in your hand. Tell the spool, "Go away!" As you say this, pull the string upward. The spool will roll away from you.

3. Next lower your hand so that the string rests on the table. Say, "Come back, spool." Pull on the string, *keeping your hand low.* This will cause the spool to roll toward you.

4. Have a member of the audience try this trick, too. The volunteer will have a hard time controlling the spool if he or she doesn't know your secret!

Balancing the Ball

This "balancing act" will astound your audience for a long time!

What You'll Need:
- A 1-foot piece of rope or cord
- A 15-inch piece of thread or thin string, the same color as the rope or cord
- A Ping-Pong ball

Getting Ready:

1. Tie each end of the thread to the corresponding ends of the rope. Don' tie them too tightly—you'll need to move the thread during the trick.

2. Be sure to practice your "balancing act" several times before performing

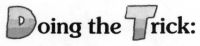

Doing the Trick:

1. Put the rope on the show table. Show the Ping-Pong ball to your audience and say, "I will now magically balance this ball on this rope."

2. Keeping the ball in your hand, pick up the rope and hold one end in each hand. The thread should be between the rope and your body. *Make sure your audience doesn't see the thread.*

3. Stretch the rope between your hands until it is straight.

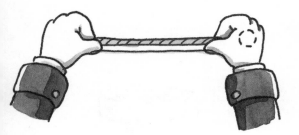

4. With your thumbs, move the thread away from the rope toward you and hold it there. *Again, make sure your audience can't see the thread.* The rope and thread together will form a little "hammock" to hold the ball.

5. Work the ball out of your hand and onto the rope and thread. The ball will be held up by the rope and thread. But to your audience, it will look as though the ball were balancing only on the rope!

Charming the String

Don't try this trick when it's raining—it works best on a dry day, when the humidity is low.

What You'll Need:

- A 3-foot piece of thread or lightweight string (waxed or plastic-coated string will not work)
- A balloon
- Tape

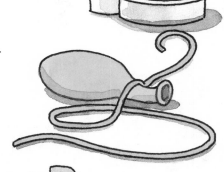

Getting Ready:

1. Blow up the balloon and tie a knot at the end.

Doing the Trick:

1. Set the balloon on your show table. Tape one end of the string to the table. Pile most of the string over the taped end, and stretch the other end.

2. Tell your audience, "This balloon will serve as the moon, and when the moon is overhead, my string becomes charmed and rises."

3. Now pick up the balloon. Close your eyes and rub the balloon against your sweater or the back of your head. The rubbing will charge the balloon with static electricity.

4. Open your eyes and hold the balloon about ¼ of an inch over the loose end of the string. The string will magically rise and attach itself to the balloon! Slowly lift the balloon, and the string will follow!

Soap on a Rope

What You'll Need:

- ▲ A thin rope or cord about 5 feet long
- ▲ Masking tape
- ▲ A bath-size bar of soap (Ivory works best)
- ▲ A sharp paring knife

Getting Ready:

1. Have an adult help you cut a hole through the middle of the soap.

2. Put one end of the rope through the hole. Then take the same end, bring it around to the bottom of the soap, and put it through the hole again. Tie the ends of the rope together.

Doing the Trick:

1. Show the soap on the rope to your audience. Say, "See this soap on a rope? I'm going to show you how to make your own soap on a rope."

2. Untie the rope from the soap. Hold the soap up in your left hand and the rope in your right hand. Say, "All you need is a bar of soap and a good rope."

3. Put one end of the rope through the hole and pull it through halfway. Let the ends hang down. Say, "All you have to do is tie the rope onto the soap like this." *Do the next four steps as quickly as possible.*

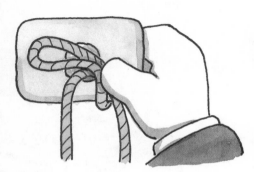

4. With your right hand, take the front piece of rope and bring it up to the back of the soap. *Be sure to form a loop.* Use your thumb to hold the loop against the back of the soap.

5. Put the back piece of rope over the loop and through the hole from back to front.

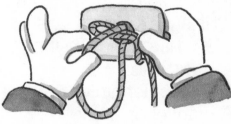

6. Tie the ends together over the soap to form a loop big enough to go over your head.

7. Put the rope around your neck so that the soap hangs with the front to your audience. Say, "It's just that easy!"

8. Then, with a puzzled look on your face, say, "But what if you want to wash your feet? The soap won't reach." Then smile and say, "Alakazam, alakazeet! I need this soap to wash my feet!" Pull the soap to your right with a quick tug. It will come off the rope!

The Great Escape

WATCH OUT HOUDINI!
HERE I COME!

Turn your trusty assistant into an expert escape artist!

What You'll Need:

- A large canvas laundry bag that ties closed and is big enough for an assistant to fit in (THE BAG MUST BE LOOSELY WOVEN FOR EASY BREATHING WHEN INSIDE. ALSO, NEVER USE A PLASTIC BAG!)
- A 10-foot length of rope or cord
- A blanket or sheet

Getting Ready:

1. Remove the cord that comes with the laundry bag and replace it with the 10-foot rope. Make a loop inside the bag with the rope, as shown.

2. Practice this trick many times with your assistant!

Doing the Trick:

1. Hold up the laundry bag and announce to your audience, "I have here an ordinary laundry bag." Introduce your assistant and say, "I will now tie up my assistant in the bag."

2. Help your assistant into the bag. Your assistant will know to step on the end of the rope as soon as he or she gets into the bag.

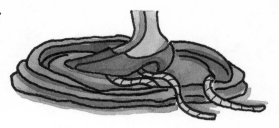

3. Have a volunteer from the audience come onstage. Ask the volunteer to *loosely* tie the bag closed. *Make sure your assistant steps hard on the looped end of the rope so that it doesn't pull out when the volunteer ties the bag.*

4. Hold up the blanket in front of the bag so that the audience cannot see the bag. Say, "I will now enable my assistant to escape by saying these magic words: Hocus pocus, zippidy zick. Help my assistant do this trick! Hocus pocus, zippidy zag. Come, assistant, out of the bag!" *If your assistant needs more time than this, make up some more magic words beforehand.*

5. While you are talking, your assistant steps off the looped end, opens the laundry bag, and climbs out. Then the assistant quickly tightens the bag closed, making sure the loop of rope is put inside the bag again.

6. Lower the blanket to show your smiling assistant holding up the tied bag!

Talking Totem

What You'll Need:

- An empty paper towel tube
- 3 small plastic rings or key rings
- A 12-inch piece and a 16-inch piece of thin string
- Markers or poster paint
- A paper clip   ▪ A paintbrush

Getting Ready:

1. Color the outside of the paper towel tube to make it look like a totem pole

2. Tie a ring to each end of the 12-inch string. Tie the third ring to one end of the 16-inch string and the paper clip to the other end.

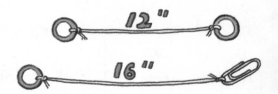

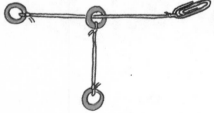

3. Pull the paper clip through one of the rings on the 12-inch string.

4. Hold the two ends of the 16-inch string together. The 12-inch string will hang from it. Then slide both strings into one end of your totem pole and out the other end. One end of the 12-inch string should stick out of the bottom.

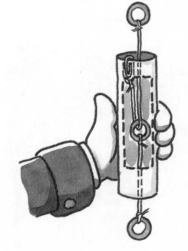

5. Clip the paper clip onto the top edge of the totem pole so that the knot is hidden inside the tube.

Doing the Trick:

1. First slip the middle finger of your left hand through the ring at the bottom of your totem pole. Rest the totem pole in your left hand.

2. Slip the middle finger of your right hand through the ring at the top end of the totem pole.

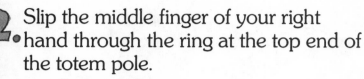

3. Show the totem pole to the audience and say, "This is a magic talking totem pole. It can answer my questions by moving up and down. When the totem moves up, that means 'yes.' When the totem moves down, that means 'no.'"

4. Ask your magic totem pole, "Can you really talk?" Slowly move your hands apart, and the totem will rise from your left hand.

5. Then ask the totem pole, "Are you enjoying the show?" Slowly move your hands farther apart and the totem will rise higher.

6. Ask the totem pole, "Am I the best magician in the world?" Slowly move your hands back together. The totem pole will fall! Your audience will laugh because it answered no!

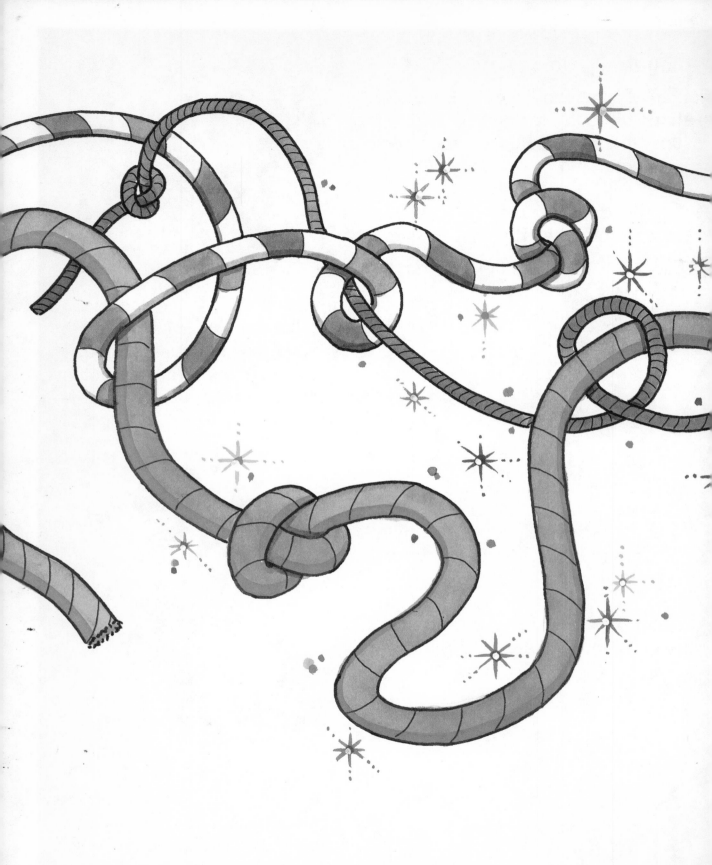